The Greedy Devotee

Adapted from Satsangs of Sant Ram Singh Ji on August 5, 2015 & January 10, 2017

Illustrated by Carlos Brito

GO JOLLY BOOKS

The Greedy Devotee

The Greedy Devotee is a story originally told in Satsangs of Sant Ram Singh Ji
on August 5, 2015 & January 10, 2017
during Meditation Retreat Programs at RadhaSwami Ashram,
Channasandra Village, Karnataka, India.

Special thanks to those who reviewed & critiqued the story:

Translated by Ashok Shinkar
Transcribed by Ali Czernin, Geoff Halstead, & Harvey Rosenberg

Go Jolly Books is blessed to have the services of Carlos Brito as illustrator and formatter; his skills make each book a special work of art. Carlos has a knack for using color in magical ways. His whimsical characters often help
to transmit the strong messages of Sant Ram Singh Ji's words to sink
deeper into our hearts and minds.

ISBN: 978-1-942937-20-3

(c) 2017 All Rights Reserved

Published by
Go Jolly Books
www.gojollybooks.com
500 Fasola Rd., Sequim, WA 98382 USA

FIRST EDITION, GO JOLLY BOOKS, First Printing 2017
10 9 8 7 6 5 4 3 2 1 Printed in the U.S.A.

The Greedy Devotee

Adapted from Satsangs of Sant Ram Singh Ji on August 5, 2015 & January 10, 2017

INTRODUCTION

In January, 2014, Sant Ram Singh Ji gave me permission to take stories He told in Satsang and publish them as books for children. This meant I could change His original words directed to adults to words more suitable for children.
With His Limitless Grace, reviewers of the first eight books have told us children like the books.

In January, 2017, He further stated: "By reading these books, children are deeply impressed and their minds start thinking of the Saints and Their preachings in such stories. Thus, the mind gets attuned towards searching for a spiritual path. Because of their sincerity and devotion, God Almighty helps them.
He brings them close to a fully attained Master,
and brings them on the path of spirituality and salvation."

The Greedy Devotee shows the importance of listening to and accepting what one's guru or Master says. As hard as it is to truly accept, on a day to day basis, that our Master knows best, when we don't listen to Him, life painfully teaches us the Reality that, in fact, our Master does know best. When we fail to obey His words, we end up like the devotee in this story.

Carlos Brito's beautiful illustrations complement the words in a fun, whimsical and beautiful way which might make it easier to deepen our trust and love for our Master, Who always has our best interests at heart.
We hope you enjoy this story book.

Radhasoami,
Harvey Rosenberg

Dedication

Sant Ram Singh Ji, a Sant Mat Master, continues to shower His Limitless Grace
that allow us to produce story books appreciated by children and adults.
We are grateful to Sant Ram Singh Ji, for without His Grace, we would never
escape the clutches of our minds and would be just like the devotee
in this book, whose greed imprisoned him.

There once was a devotee who followed a rishi and did his seva.

After ten years, he asked the rishi if he could return home to visit his family.

The rishi appreciated the seva done by the devotee. Because the devotee was poor and had difficulty providing food and clothing for his family, the rishi wanted to shower grace on him.
So, he gave him four candles.

The rishi then instructed him, "Take these candles and go home. When everyone is asleep, light one candle and go eastwards. Dig at the place where the candle burns out, and you will find some coins.

Then, the next day, light the second candle and go northwards. When this candle burns out, stop and dig there. You will discover a pot with more coins.

On the third day, light the third candle, and go westwards. When this candle burns out, stop and dig. You will find a pot of precious jewels.

But don't light this fourth candle and don't go southwards."

The devotee was thrilled and took the four candles. When he reached home, he thought, "Why wait for four days to burn the candles? Let me light all the candles, go in all four directions and whatever I get,
I'll become rich in only one day."

When nightfall arrived, he lit the first candle and walked eastwards. After an hour, the candle burned out. He dug there, and found a pot of rupees.

He quickly returned home, lit the next candle, and went northwards. He walked about half a kilometer when the second candle burned out. He dug there and found a pot of gold and silver coins.

He returned home a happy man.

But he was impatient to light the third candle. He said, "I will not wait any longer." So, he lit the third candle and went westwards.

After walking for almost one kilometer, the third candle burned out. He dug there and found a large pot of diamonds.

He took the diamonds, and was thoroughly pleased. In his mind he thanked the rishi. He felt, "I worked for him for ten years, and appreciate the reward he has given me. My poverty is now gone as a result of his grace."

But he still had the fourth candle. He began wondering why the rishi had told him not to light that candle. "Perhaps, if I light this candle and go southwards, I will reach the den of Kubera, the god of wealth, himself."

"Okay, let's not miss out on this opportunity," he said to himself as he lit the candle and walked to the south. After half a kilometer, the candle burned out, and he started digging.

He dug about five feet, but didn't find anything. When he dug further, his shovel hit something hard, like cement or concrete. He thought it might be the roof of a house.

He was thrilled and quite sure he had found Kubera's house. So, he dug further and found a door.

The devotee replied, "Okay, can you show me the way to the treasure?"

The man answered, "Can't you see I have a lot of weight on my head? It's very difficult for me to talk like this. If you would hold the ceiling for me for a few moments, I'll tell you."

The devotee agreed. "Sure, I'll hold it for you."

He put his head under the ceiling and relieved the man.

"Now, show me the way to the treasure," the excited devotee stated.

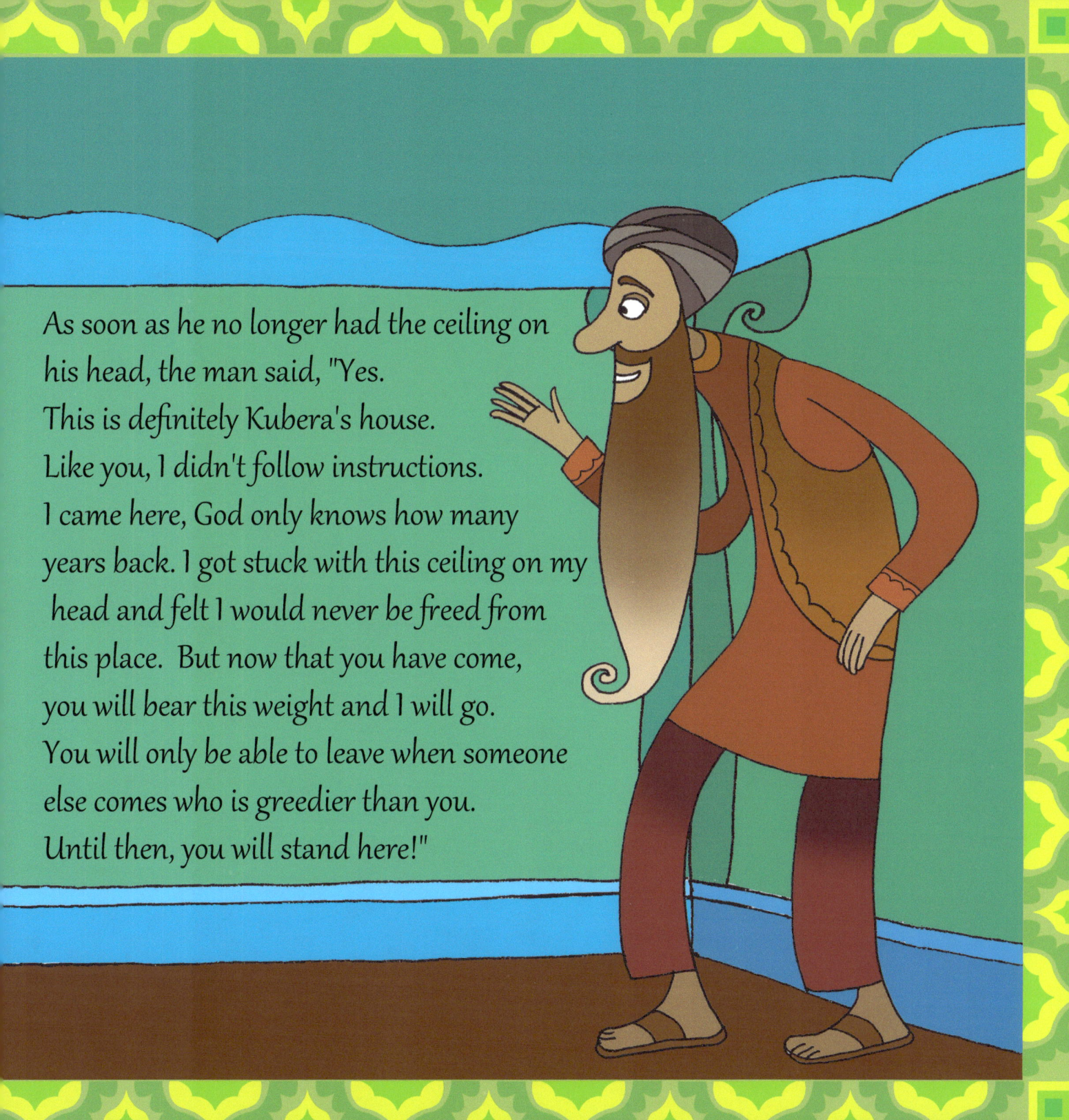

It is greed that is the undoing of a person. If he has a few crores, he wants more. If he gets ten crores, he wants a hundred crores. Because he always wants more and more, he remains hollow and sad.

Swami Ji Maharaj says, "Just like that monkey, which gets caught by himself in greed, similarly, Kal and Maya have kept this vice of greed in a human being. And he also is entangled here, because of that."